Great Artists
Michelangelo

W9-AXZ-077

ABDO
Publishing Company

Joanne Mattern

visit us at
www.abdopub.com

Published by ABDO Publishing Company, 4940 Viking Drive, Edina, Minnesota 55435.
Copyright © 2005 by Abdo Consulting Group, Inc. International copyrights reserved in all countries. No part of this book may be reproduced in any form without written permission from the publisher. The Checkerboard Library™ is a trademark and logo of ABDO Publishing Company.

Printed in the United States.

Cover Photo: Getty Images
Interior Photos: Art Resource pp. 13, 18, 20; Corbis pp. 5, 9, 11, 12, 14, 15, 17, 19, 21, 23, 25, 27, 29; Getty Images p. 1

Series Coordinator: Megan Murphy
Editors: Heidi M. Dahmes, Megan Murphy
Cover Design: Neil Klinepier
Interior Design: Dave Bullen

Library of Congress Cataloging-in-Publication Data

Mattern, Joanne, 1963-
    Michelangelo / Joanne Mattern.
        p. cm. -- (Great artists)
    Includes index.
    ISBN 1-59197-845-9
    1. Michelangelo Buonarroti, 1475-1564--Juvenile literature. 2. Artists--Italy--Biography--Juvenile literature. I. Title.

N6923.B9M366 2005
709'.2--dc22
[B]
                                                                    2004052807

Contents

Michelangelo

Michelangelo di Lodovico Buonarroti Simoni is one of the greatest artists of all time. He lived in Italy more than 400 years ago. But, his art is still admired and respected today. Many of his works are still in Florence and Rome. They are enjoyed by visitors from around the world.

Michelangelo lived during the **Renaissance**. This was a time of great change, especially in art. Many artists at that time painted religious scenes. Michelangelo's religious faith is evident in his sculptures and paintings. His appreciation of the human form is clearly expressed in his works, too.

Michelangelo's true love was sculpture. But, he was also a master of painting, drawing, poetry, and even **architecture**. Michelangelo was passionate about every project he worked on.

Michelangelo is remembered for his ambitious projects. Many of his works are among the most famous in the world.

1475 ~ Michelangelo di Lodovico Buonarroti Simoni was born in Caprese, Italy, on March 6.

1488 ~ On April 1, Michelangelo was officially apprenticed to the Ghirlandajo brothers.

1491 ~ Michelangelo carved *Madonna of the Stairs*.

1492 ~ Michelangelo finished *Battle of the Centaurs*.

1499 ~ Michelangelo's *Pietà* was finished.

1504 ~ After almost three years of labor, Michelangelo finished *David* for the Florence cathedral.

1512 ~ Michelangelo completed the frescoes for the Sistine Chapel's ceiling.

1534 ~ Michelangelo left Florence for the last time.

1541 ~ Michelangelo finished *The Last Judgment*.

1564 ~ On February 18, Michelangelo died in Rome, Italy.

Fun Facts

- During Michelangelo's time, there was no government postal service. Letters had to be privately delivered. Because of this, many letters were lost. When Michelangelo had something important to send, he would write two letters to be carried off at different times.

- *Pietà* is Italian for "mercy."

- Michelangelo's marble *Pietà* was damaged on May 21, 1972. Australian geologist Lazlo Toth hit the statue with a hammer while crying, "I am Jesus Christ."

- It is said that St. Peter's Basilica is built where Saint Peter, one of Jesus Christ's apostles and considered the first pope, was either killed or buried. Saint Peter's tomb lies beneath the church's main altar. Other popes have been buried in the basilica, too.

Family

Michelangelo was born in Caprese, Italy, on March 6, 1475. His full name was Michelangelo di Lodovico Buonarroti Simoni. He was the second of five boys.

Michelangelo's father, Lodovico, had been from a prominent family in Florence. But, Michelangelo's grandfather had lost their money. Lodovico was a proud man. He wanted money and power. But, he did not want to work for it.

Shortly before Michelangelo was born, Lodovico served as mayor of Caprese. The family lived in Caprese for six months. When Michelangelo was less than a month old, they moved back to Florence.

Michelangelo's mother, Francesca, was a **frail** woman. She could not take care of him. So, Michelangelo did not go to Florence with them. Instead, he stayed with a family of stonemasons in the nearby village of Settignano. Francesca died when Michelangelo was six years old.

Florence, Italy

Back Home

When Michelangelo was 10 years old, his father remarried. Lodovico decided it was time for Michelangelo to come home. When Michelangelo moved to Florence, he began his schooling. But, he did not like to study. He wanted to draw.

Michelangelo had a friend who was **apprenticed** to an artist named Domenico Ghirlandajo. Ghirlandajo was one of the most respected artists in Florence at that time. Michelangelo's friend secretly took drawings for Michelangelo to copy.

Eventually, Michelangelo told his father he wanted to be an artist. Lodovico was very angry at his son. Lodovico wanted Michelangelo to get a job and make lots of money. He thought an artist was not a respectable position.

After many arguments, Lodovico gave up. When Michelangelo was 13 years old, his father sent him to be Ghirlandajo's apprentice.

Artist's Corner

Michelangelo

Michelangelo used the true fresco medium. He most likely was exposed to this technique by Domenico Ghirlandajo. In fresco painting, wet plaster is applied to a surface. The artist then paints while the plaster is still wet. Often, many layers of paint must be applied in order to achieve rich colors.

The fresco's design is usually planned out before the project is begun. After the plaster is applied, the design is transferred onto the surface using a cartoon. A cartoon contains the full-scale drawing of the finished design on tracing paper.

Michelangelo applied his designs to the plaster by holding up the paper and tracing the lines with a stylus. When he first began, he followed the lines exactly. As time went on, he was freer with his design.

Detail of **Angel Appearing to Zacharias** *by Domenico Ghirlandajo. Ghirlandajo was famous for his frescoes. Michelangelo's Sistine Chapel frescoes display the influence of Ghirlandajo's style.*

Art Apprentice

On April 1, 1488, Michelangelo was officially **apprenticed** to Domenico Ghirlandajo and his brothers for three years. But, Michelangelo was unsatisfied with the brothers because they refused to teach him. He left after only one year.

During his apprenticeship, Michelangelo had snuck away and discovered the gardens at the Monastery of San Marco. Sculptor Bertoldo di Giovanni was in charge of the gardens. Before officially leaving his apprenticeship, Michelangelo had begun secretly studying under Bertoldo.

At that time, Lorenzo de Medici was the ruler of Florence. Lorenzo loved art. And, he had brought many ancient Greek and Roman statues to the gardens.

Lorenzo was called the Magnificent.

One day, Lorenzo saw young Michelangelo carving a **faun**. Lorenzo commented that the old-looking faun had too many teeth. When he returned later, Michelangelo had improved the statue. Lorenzo liked Michelangelo's work so much that he took him to live in his palace.

A sculpture by Bertoldo di Giovanni. Michelangelo developed his own sculpting style under Bertoldo.

The Medicis

When Michelangelo entered the Medici palace, he studied freely under Bertoldo. The Medicis treated Michelangelo very well. However, Michelangelo did not have many friends. He often made fun of other artists. One day, another **apprentice** punched Michelangelo and broke his nose!

Michelangelo continued sculpting under Bertoldo. In 1491, Michelangelo carved a sculpture called *Madonna of the Stairs*. The next year he finished the *Battle of the Centaurs*. These are the only remaining marble works from his apprenticeship days.

Madonna of the Stairs

Lorenzo de Medici died in 1492. Michelangelo was saddened by his death. But he continued creating art. However, Lorenzo's oldest son, Piero, became ruler of Florence. And, Piero did not like Michelangelo.

Battle of the Centaurs

Soon, Michelangelo went back to his father's house. He wanted to master human **anatomy**. So, he began **dissecting** dead bodies. Anatomy influenced his work from then on.

Pietà

Piero was a terrible ruler. In 1494, the Medicis were overthrown, and Piero fled Florence. Girolamo Savonarola overtook the city. Savonarola was a powerful man who preached against the Medicis. He promised to remove dishonesty from the government and the church.

Michelangelo feared Savonarola's power. So he left for Venice, and then Bologna. In Bologna, Michelangelo carved three marble statues for Saint Dominic's tomb. Then in 1496, Michelangelo traveled to Rome.

In Rome, a French cardinal commissioned Michelangelo to carve a pietà. A pietà is a piece of art that shows the Virgin Mary holding the dead Jesus Christ on her lap. The sculpture was meant for the cardinal's tomb chapel in St. Peter's Basilica.

Michelangelo's *Pietà* was completed in 1499. This was one of the few works Michelangelo signed. He later regretted it. Michelangelo said he would never sign another piece again.

Michelangelo's Pietà *is now housed in St. Peter's Basilica in Rome.*

Another Success

Savonarola's rule had ended in 1498. Michelangelo returned to Florence in 1501. The Florentines were happy to see the famous artist and sculptor. Michelangelo soon began his next great work.

That year, Michelangelo was asked to create a sculpture for the cathedral of Florence. For the project, he received an 18-foot (6-m) block of marble that had already been used. Michelangelo carved a figure of David, a hero from the Bible. He worked for about three years in secrecy.

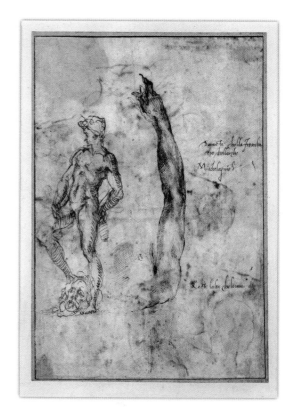

Drawings for the marble David

Finally in September 1504, Michelangelo's *David* was shown to the public. People loved the mighty statue. It showed a brave, young hero.

David stood as a symbol of Florence's independence. And, it established Michelangelo as the leading Florentine artist. It is still considered one of the world's greatest statues.

In 1505, Michelangelo started another large job. He was to carve the 12 **apostles** for the Florence cathedral. But he only started on one. Leaving works unfinished was a common practice for Michelangelo.

Michelangelo's **David** *stands in the Accademia Museum in Florence.*

Love of Work

Michelangelo saw each project as a problem to solve. However, he was more interested in the problem than in the completed piece. Michelangelo quit a project when he saw a mistake. Then he began a new one. He stopped many projects before they were finished.

Despite his many unfinished works, Michelangelo's popularity was increasing. He was wealthy and supported his father, brothers, and nephews. His brothers and father were greedy and irresponsible. But, Michelangelo had strong loyalties toward all his family.

One of many unfinished sculptures started by Michelangelo

Hidden Treasure

Michelangelo eventually turned his back on the Medici family. At one point in his career, Michelangelo worked with the city of Florence to improve its defenses. Florence was attempting to keep the Medicis out of power with a war.

Florence's efforts did not work. The Medicis regained control. Then, Michelangelo was charged with treason and ordered to be killed. So in 1530, Michelangelo hid in a room under the Medici Chapel for six weeks.

While in hiding, Michelangelo covered the walls with drawings and sketches. These were found by Paolo Dal Poggetto in 1975. Michelangelo left about 50 drawings behind, including a self-portrait.

Michelangelo also had friendships that he valued deeply. Whenever Michelangelo left Florence, he was saddened to leave behind his beloved family and friends.

Michelangelo enjoyed spending time with friends. But, he loved to work more than anything else. When he was working, he often did not stop to eat or sleep. He lived a simple life and was always absorbed in his work.

Pope's Orders

Pope Julius II soon heard about Michelangelo's work. Pope Julius wanted a tomb designed for himself. So, he asked Michelangelo to come to Rome and take on the project.

Michelangelo planned a huge, three-**tiered** tomb that included 40 statues. But soon after Michelangelo started, Pope Julius lost interest in the project.

Pope Julius stopped payment on the tomb. Michelangelo asked to be paid for the work he had already done. But, Pope Julius refused to talk to him.

Feeling like he had wasted his time, Michelangelo left Rome and returned to Florence. This made Pope Julius angry. He had not given Michelangelo permission to leave.

Pope Julius pressured Florence's government to send Michelangelo back. Finally, Michelangelo gave in. And, he was put to work in Bologna on a bronze statue of Pope Julius.

Michelangelo did not want this job. But, he had to follow Pope Julius's orders. When Michelangelo finished the sculpture, Pope Julius assigned him another unpleasant job. But, it became one of Michelangelo's greatest achievements.

Michelangelo spent months choosing the marble for Pope Julius's tomb. Forty years after he began, only a few statues were completed.

Sistine Chapel

Pope Julius wanted Michelangelo to fresco the Sistine Chapel's ceiling in Rome. The Sistine Chapel was the pope's own chapel. And, it was where the cardinals met to elect a new pope. It was a beautiful and important place.

Michelangelo did not want to paint the ceiling. He told Pope Julius he was a sculptor, not a painter. But Pope Julius would not listen. Finally, Michelangelo started the job.

Michelangelo completed the job almost entirely by himself. However, one man laid the plaster and another ground and mixed the paints. Each day, a fresh layer of plaster was laid over a part of the ceiling. Michelangelo painted that section while the plaster was still wet. He could not repaint mistakes.

Michelangelo completed the huge job in less than four years. He painted in the hot, dry summer. Paint dripped down on Michelangelo's face. He barely took time to eat or sleep.

Michelangelo finished the ceiling in 1512. He had painted the biblical story of the Creation. The nine main scenes portray the story of Genesis from the Creation to the Flood.

Many believe the Sistine Chapel ceiling is one of the most beautiful paintings in the world. This scene shows Michelangelo's version of the Creation of Adam.

Last Judgment

For the next 20 years, Michelangelo lived and worked in Florence. He created the Medici Chapel and the Laurentian Library to honor the Medici family. He also wrote poetry.

In 1534, Michelangelo left Florence for the last time. He went to Rome to work for Pope Paul III. Pope Paul wanted Michelangelo to fresco the wall behind the Sistine Chapel's main altar.

Michelangelo began a fresco called *The Last Judgment*. Michelangelo's painting style had changed over the years. His colors were now simple, with brown bodies against a blue sky. And, the figures are less energetic.

Michelangelo finished *The Last Judgment* in 1541. The painting includes hundreds of figures waiting for God to decide if they should go to heaven. It is a violent, frightening piece of art.

The painting stirred up strong emotions. A lot of people did not like that many of the figures were not wearing clothes. But,

In the early 1990s, **The Last Judgment** *was restored to its original beauty with a four-year cleaning. After much discussion, the Vatican allowed restorers to remove most of the articles of clothing that had been added by other artists.*

Michelangelo did not care what people thought. Other artists were later hired to cover the images. The painting that was once disapproved of by many is now admired.

Last Triumph

In his last years, Michelangelo was named the chief **architect** of the New St. Peter's Basilica. Michelangelo was old and sick when he worked on St. Peter's. But even in his old age, he was a hard worker.

Michelangelo planned the church. He also designed the dome. Many people consider St. Peter's dome to be the finest architectural achievement of the Italian **Renaissance**.

Michelangelo died on February 18, 1564, in Rome. He never married or had children. Michelangelo left his nephew instructions to bury him in Florence next to his father. His body remained in Rome for two weeks. He was then moved to his hometown and buried.

Michelangelo lived during a time when many great pieces of art were created. Many artists from the Renaissance are still remembered today. But Michelangelo rises above them all. He is truly one of the greatest painters and sculptors the world has ever known.

St. Peter's Basilica is considered one of the largest churches ever built. It can hold 60,000 people and covers 247,570 square feet (23,000 sq m).

Glossary

anatomy - a branch of science that deals with the structure of animals or plants and the relationship of their parts.

apostle - any early Christian leader, especially the original 12 selected by Jesus Christ to preach his word.

apprentice - a person who learns a trade or craft from a skilled worker.

architecture - the art of planning and designing buildings. A person who designs architecture is called an architect.

dissect - to separate into parts for the purpose of studying.

faun - a Roman mythology character with the body of a man and the ears, horns, legs, and tail of a goat.

frail - weak and easily sick.

Renaissance - a revival of art and learning that began in Italy during the fourteenth century, marked by a renewed interest in Greek and Latin literature and art.

tier - one of two or more layers or rows arranged together.

Saying It

Bologna - boh-LOH-nyah
Domenico Ghirlandajo - doh-MAY-nee-koh gihr-lahn-DEYE-oh
Girolamo Savonarola - jee-RAW-lahm-oh sah-voh-nah-RAW-lah
Lorenzo de Medici - loh-REHNT-soh day MEHD-ee-chee
Michelangelo di Lodovico Buonarroti Simoni -
mee-kay-LAHN-jay-loh dee loh-doh-VEE-koh bwaw-nahr-RAW-tee see-MOH-nee
Settignano - seht-TEENYAH-noh

Web Sites

To learn more about Michelangelo, visit ABDO Publishing Company on the World Wide Web at **www.abdopub.com**. Web sites about Michelangelo are featured on our Book Links page. These links are routinely monitored and updated to provide the most current information available.

Index